David Rankin, Farmer

D Rankin

David Rankin
„ Farmer „

Modern Agricultural Methods Con-
trasted with Primitive Agricultural
Methods by the Life History
of a Plain Farmer

More Corn Grown on His Farm Last Year Than in the
Nine States—Utah, Oregon, Washington, Arizona, Idaho
Montana, Rhode Island, Wyoming and Nevada combined

TARKIO, MISSOURI, U. S. A.

FOREWORD

Agriculture is basic. Upon it rests cities and commerce and civilization. There are great men who lead armies in war or regiments in peace, who succeed in business or statecraft, who write songs or make laws, who add to human knowledge or subtract from human misery—and the stories of their lives are interesting and inspiring. How much more inspiring and interesting is the story of the life of the farmer upon whose success depends all the other industries and activities of man. To tell the story of the life of a plain farmer, David Rankin, humbly born, but of heroic type—to set down in his own simple straightforward speech, the secret of his great career as inspiration to farmers everywhere this book is written.

Made Millions Farming

I was born in Sullivan county, Indiana, May 28, 1825. My father was of Scotch-Irish descent, who came to this country early in the 17th century; my mother a Quaker, both of very limited means. BORN IN INDIANA 84 YEARS AGO

In 1831, when I was six years old, my father left Sullivan county, Indiana, and moved to Park county, Indiana. Father was a very straight-walking man and he said that Sullivan county was too wicked a place in which to raise a family. FATHER MOVES BECAUSE COUNTY TOO WICKED FOR RAISING FAMILY Park county was situated in a fine timber country. Here he moved within the limits of the Associate Reformed Presbyterian church. Father belonged to the old Scotch Division, known as the Associate Reformed Presbyterian church. My mother's father came out ahead of us and he entered a great deal of land in Sullivan and Vermillion counties. He was a gun maker by trade and made guns for the soldiers for the War of 1812.

Father went back again to the old home place in Indiana, near Fairbanks, a year or two afterwards, and traded for 200 acres that my grandfather had entered. There was a little 16 feet square log cabin on it and we went to LIVED IN 16 FT. SQ. LOG CABIN live in this cabin. These cabins or log houses were quite comfortable. They were rough logs inside and outside. They were notched at the ends and laid one

on top of each other, which made a lock-joint. They were almost storm proof, an ordinary cyclone would have a good job in moving one of them. The cracks between the logs were carefully chinked up with mortar, and the chimney which rose above a great fireplace in one end, was made of wood strips and clay. Most of the cooking was done in a large pot or kettle on the fireplace. The kettle had to be watched that it did not upset as it rested on top of the logs. The meals were simple in those days, consisting mostly of tame and wild meats, fresh in the winter time, and of smoked meats and pickled side meat, or salt pork as we called it in the summer time. Our meat was smoked with genuine old fashioned "hickory" smoke in those days, and not by chemicals as is mostly done now. The bread was cooked in a Dutch oven with coals under it and coals on top.

SMOKE MEAT IS GOOD NOW, BUT WAS BETTER THEN

Maybe we had to work harder to get it, but somehow the ham nowadays don't smell quite so fragrant or taste quite so rich and satisfying as it seemed to then. You know, I believe we appreciated everything we got in those days, because we didn't have so many luxuries. The ordinary laborer lives higher now than most of the rich class did in those days.

When we got fixed up in our new cabin, we were ready to commence in earnest.

There was a patch of about 20 acres where the cattle had eaten off the wild grass. Father broke this up and put it in corn and here raised the biggest crop he had ever raised.

We lived in this new locality three years

Home Farm of David Rankin. Showing House and Barn In Foreground.

and then moved out to Warren county, Illinois (now Henderson county), in March, 1836. We were about a month going from Indiana to Illinois, traveling every day. The trip was made overland with teams, a distance of about 250 miles. The horses would get stuck in the mud and, had it not been for the oxen we had along, and the oxen of our neighbors who were moving with us, we could not have finished our journey on account of the mud. There were no fences in the country and the houses were twenty to thirty miles apart. There were no bridges and we had to ford the streams.

CROSSED ILLINOIS RIVER IN FLAT BOAT, REQUIRING TWO DAYS
WHILE WAITING FOR BOAT HIS ONLY CHANCE TO GO FISHING

At that time there were only a few houses in Bloomington and Peoria. We had to cross the Illinois river at Peoria in a flatboat. Having to wait our turn, it took us two days to get across. This was about the only chance I ever had to go fishing.

We had no matches in those days and had to make a fire with the flintrock. I remember also seeing father start a fire with

FIRE WITHOUT MATCHES

a little hand grain sickle, by putting powder on a Dutch oven lid and striking the lid with the sickle, using tow to catch fire from the powder. I have carried fire a mile from neighbor's when our fire was out at home. I was sixteen years old before I saw a match. It seems strange now to think that there ever was a time when there was no matches, now when you can buy enough matches for a nickel to last the ordinary family a month, and some careful and saving ones possibly two or three months. They tell me there is enough matches made and used in the United States every day to require 3500 cords

An Early Morning Start From the Home Barn.

of wood. And it seems that in everything else we are about as reckless and wasteful with our timber. Think of the millions of tons of wood which goes into newspapers. I think the newspapers are a great thing, but surely a part of the paper used for this purpose is absolutely wasted. Is it any wonder that we are getting concerned about where the future supply of paper is to come from. They tell me that there is good prospects that they'll be paying us farmers a nice round price for our corn stalks to make paper of before many years, and they say that corn stalks make good paper, too.

WILL USE OUR CORN STALKS FOR MAKING PAPER

My father built and operated a saw mill in Henderson county, Illinois, in 1837, and all of us children were drafted for work at the mill. As my father, being in poor health, was able to make only small profit from his mill, we had only clothing made of homespun cloth from the raw wool and flax. I was brought up in poverty and privation.

WORE HOMESPUN CLOTHING AND LIVED IN HOUSE WITH GREASED PAPER WINDOWS

The only schools we had in those days were little subscription schools, held in log houses, with windows of greased paper. We had only greased paper windows in my home. The principal studies taught us were the three R's: Reading, 'Riting, and 'Rithmetic. I had a very limited opportunity to get these prime essentials of an education. I expect the hard way in which I got them made them

Bank and Office.

10

more beneficial to me than if I had had the easier facilities of learning that the boys of today have. I quit school at the LOG SCHOOL HOUSE UNTIL 11 YEARS OLD—THEN WENT TO WORK age of eleven years and went to work to help support the family. Living in those days was on a different basis entirely from the life of today. A good education was not looked upon as so essential as now. Shoes were plentiful, but cash was so scarce that the common people could little more than afford shoes for the cold weather, for we had no money with which to buy them, and the most of them were home made. I went barefooted every WENT BAREFOOTED UNTIL 28 YEARS OLD summer until I was 28 years of age. The plain way of living which we practiced in those days gave people a much stronger constitution than the strenuous living of today.

About 1840, in order to pay a store debt for father, I hauled dressed hogs to Oquawka, Illinois, on the Mississippi river, and sold them at $1.00 to $1.25 a hundred. SOLD DRESSED HOGS AT ONE DOLLAR A HUNDRED TO PAY FATHER'S STORE DEBT The corn these hogs were fattened on was cultivated with a single shovel plow and the ground plowed with a wooden mouldboard. With these plows you had to carry a paddle and clean the plow about every twenty rods. A good team PLOWED WITH WOODEN MOULDBOARD PLOW DRAWN BY OXEN of oxen would plow about an acre each day.

It is said that "good plowing" is the first thing necessary to good farm work, and

"Wood Mouldboard Plow."

I know that it is, but when I look back and see how crude our tools were and how poor the plowing was in those days, I wonder that we raised half as much as we did. Of course our land was new and rich, and we did not have so many weeds to fight. We had to do a great deal of hoe work in those days. They were great big hoes, one of them would weigh as much as four or five of the kind of steel hoes which we use now. Well, sir, it's mighty hard to appreciate what the steel plow has done for America, surely we never could have reached what we have accomplished in Agriculture without it. Farmers nowadays don't appreciate it, they can't, because they have never had to put up with the old kind of home-made tools. Why, some of our farmers are not too overindustrious with what we've got now.

HARD TO APPRECIATE WHAT STEEL PLOW HAS DONE

There were lots of deer everywhere, and many other varieties of wild game. It was a rare thing to go out in the open prairie any-

Now Kept as Pets. Destroyed His Wheat When Mr. Rankin Began Farming in Illinois.

where without seeing some deer. I picked up lots of flint arrow points that had been shot by the Indians. They were always on rolling land, as the Indian could not get close enough to the game on the level land.

You see the Indians, or most of them had been pushed on west by the time that father moved out to Illinois. There was occasionally a roving band, and there was an occasional skirmish out on the frontier. PLENTY OF INDIANS IN THOSE DAYS Of course they were a treacherous set, and used to keep the early settlers guessing a good deal at what to expect next, and they had to sleep with their rifles pretty handy by night time, but I wouldn't be surprised that the white man would have put up a pretty ugly fight too, if driven from his own native land. Of course, I believe in civilization and progress, and that the better things must take the place of the old, but in a good many of their scraps I expect the white man was to blame for it, and that in many cases he was just as mean as the Indian. Of course Indians never had the opportunity for education then that they now have, or that the white's have had. We now have some pretty well educated Indians in the United States, a good many in the Legislature, and one up to the United States Senate — FIRST EXPERIENCE WITH THE TARIFF all of which is but another sign of how great the achievement of our age in education as well as agriculture.

When, in 1836, we began farming in Henderson county, father built a saw mill there the next year. He paid $1.00 a day for help and got $1,000 in debt and couldn't pay a dollar of debt for six or eight years. I tell you when we got the low tariff we soon lost all we had, or nearly so. In 1836-37 was the campaign in which the saying was originated, "Free trade and sailor's rights," and we came near getting both, and the people didn't want either after they got them. They proved a very poor diet to live on. After this time, we had men to run the saw mill for $10.00 to $12.00 a month, and they boarded themselves.

SCHOOL TEACHERS PAID TWELVE DOL-
LARS A MONTH !

They took their pay in trade, as we had no money to pay them. The school teachers made only $12.00 a month and boarded themselves.

You know I have always been a great friend of the public school system of our country, and I guess I do my part in supporting them. I believe it is one of the great things which has made this country of ours so wonderfully great among the nations of this earth. I believe in a free school system that will give to every boy and girl a good sensible education, and that whether he wants it or not. I believe in compulsory education, too. The only reason a boy or girl don't appreciate it more than the average boy does, is because they can't realize how much they need it, and how much it will be worth to them in after life. Some people don't seem to think that a boy needs much of an education

WE OUGHT TO APPRECIATE EDUCA-
TION

unless he's going into business, or into some of the professions. I tell you that no young man ever had too good an education to make a successful farmer.

I want people to know that I have a warm heart for the teachers of this country, all of them, including the teachers of the little red school house at the cross-roads.

While visiting in Illinois not long ago I was talking to one of my old friends. He told me he got the high price of $13.00 a month at that time for teaching school, and boarded himself, which was after Jackson's administration. I paid $2.50 for an axe for father that was made in Sheffield, England, but I can and have bought as good an axe nowadays for seventy-five cents. We had the axe, you see, and the other fellow across the water had the money, so I have always been in favor of protective tariff. At that time we plowed the ground with wooden mould-board plow. We cut our grain with a hand sickle, and threshed the grain by tramping it out with horses, or by flay-ing it out with a flail, cleaning it up with a sheet or fanning mill. Up to this time we had made no progress since the days of Moses, cutting wheat just as Boaz did when Ruth gleaned the field after the reapers. Wheat was selling at twenty-five cents per bushel, and we got one-fourth the price for it in cash, and three-fourths of it we had to take in goods, buying calico at twenty-five cents to forty cents per yard. My uncle, who was a merchant, sold calico at forty cents a yard and bought tow linen from the same women that they had made by hand, for ten cents a yard. It was a yard wide, while calico was only about thirty inches wide.

CUT GRAIN WITH A REAP HOOK, AND THRESHED WITH A FLAIL

CALICO COST FORTY CENTS A YARD IN CALICO AGE—NOW IN THE SILK AGE

I remember hearing father tell about go-ing to mill when he lived in Washington, Pa. Oil had run out and down into the streams and caught fire and burned the tree tops. Oil in those days was considered the reliable cure for rheumatism, and their way of collecting it was to take the bed blankets and soak them in

15

the streams, then wring the blankets by hand, and thus get the oil. To get our flour,

MILL WAS OPERATED BY HORSES

we took our wheat to a mill operated by horses, and we furnished the horses, hitched to a sweep. I remember going to the mill seven times, a week apart, for our grist before I got it, going fourteen miles each trip with a yoke of oxen. During that time, we lived on potatoes and bread made from wheat, ground in a coffee mill or corn pounded out in a mortar. A laughable incident occured about this time. My father had added a grist mill to his saw mill. A neighbor came with some corn to be ground. As it was run by a water wheel, the belt, which was made of untanned cowhide, would stretch a good deal. The mill ground very slowly and as he was looking on, the neighbor made this remark: "That mill is a spunky little devil. As soon as it gets done with one grain, it hops onto another."

In those days, the mail was forwarded without postage and the one receiving the letter had to pay twenty-five cents post-

FOUR BUSHELS OF WHEAT AS POSTAGE ON A SINGLE LETTER

age to get it. It took four bushels of wheat to get a letter out of the post-office, as we could get only one-fourth in cash for wheat.

About 1844 the first plows of steel were made. These plows would scour. The

FIRST IRON MOULDBOARD—IT WOULD SCOR

first steel plow I ever heard of was at Farmington, Illinois, near Galesburg, made by hand. Shortly after that I learned that John Deere and others were making steel plows.

Father had got along pretty well, but when President Jackson vetoed the currency

16

act, he lost all he had in the saw mill enterprise, because there was no money left in the country. He traded a filley and a cow for a quarter section of land in Henderson county. The filley and cow were valued at $50.00. A man and I went out on the prairies and put in an eighty acre crop of wheat. We had a little shanty and did our own cooking. There were lots of deer around there and they troubled us a great deal by pasturing on the wheat that winter. Land was very cheap. I knew of as good a quarter section as there was in Henderson county, or any other county, selling for $30.00—not $30.00 an acre, but the whole 160 acres for $30.00—and the man traded a yoke of oxen for it, as he had no money. This was four miles from where Biggsville is now located. The land had a fine spring on it and no waste land. By that time we were using cradles for cutting wheat instead of reap hooks. We had to haul our wheat about ten miles to the Mississippi river, and sold it for forty to fifty cents per bushel. We harvested some wheat at the time of the Mexican War, cutting it with the cradle, and we got fifty cents a bushel in silver—Mexican dollars.

TRADED A QUARTER SECTION FOR ONE FILLEY AND A COW

ANOTHER QUARTER SECTION SOLD FOR THIRTY-DOLLAR YOKE OF OXEN

CRADLES SUCCEED SICKLES FOR CUTTING WHEAT

In those days, when money was so scarce, a good deal of ingenuity was used in trading. It was barter and trade sure enough. One of our neighbors bought a horse and promised to pay the money for it, intending to pay for it out of his wheat. As he was able to get only one-fourth of it in cash, he was obliged to pay the rest in trade. There was a general merchant who kept,

BARTER AND TRADE THE INVARIABLE RULE—MONEY ALMOST UNKNOWN

among other things, a line of hardware, and it happened that this man's neighbor wanted some hardware, so he let him have the hardware for the balance of the bill, and gave the other man the cash. In that way he paid for his horse.

In 1846 I was starting to do for myself, for I learned in my early boyhood days that farming was the business. All other kinds of business depended largely, if not entirely upon it, and as I was taught no other trade, I became an apprentice by birth, and I am glad of it, although I really had a desire to be a store-keeper—merchant I suppose you would call it, and made some effort to get a position as clerk several times, about the time I was of age, but I didn't find any one that thought I knew enough to make a good clerk. I had been watching the operations of Mr. Strawn, who was the only cattle feeder I knew of at that time, and I decided if I could combine the stock business with farming, i. e., make both industries one, there was a greater opportunity, and that was really the foundation of my plan to be a farmer.

I began to reason on the matter and decided it was the most independent calling, and began to plan to be a plain farmer, and with this in view decided, after careful study, to adopt farming for my life work. I had traded

lumber for bulls because I could not get as
large and strong steers or work oxen for
the price. This was in the fall, and next
spring I needed one to make up a team.
I went to a neighbor and bought one for $8.00,
weighing twelve hundred pounds, and agreed
to pay for him in work, and now I was
ready for my first plow. I went up to
Oquawka to buy iron for a plow point.
I didn't have the money and they
wouldn't sell it to me unless some one
would guarantee the bill, which amounted to
$6.00. A good friend of our family by the
name of Spears, went my security at the hardware store for this piece of iron. Father
made the wooden plow, stocked the plow, and
Mr. Spears, being a blacksmith, did the iron
work for me. This was my first purchase in
agricultural implements, and never since
have I bought as little as I did the first year.
A gentleman once asked me how much money
I had paid for agricultural implements. Of
course I couldn't tell, and I don't believe I
could figure out within many thousand dollars, the amount I have invested in agricultural implements: but I do know that, in the
main, every purchase has proven profitable.
You see, I figure this way, whenever I
can buy an implement that will reduce
the labor or perform the work better
than the old style machine, it pays me
to throw the old ones away and get the new
ones. I have always been the first, or among
the first, to get new improved machines in
the different localities where I have lived. In
reality, it isn't the cost of a machine that fig-
ures much anyway. Let me prove this to you.
Now, a good steel plow will turn two to three

BEGINNING WORK FOR HIMSELF

TRADED LUMBER FOR WORK BULLS

HIS FIRST PURCHASE IN AGRICULTUR-
AL IMPLEMENTS

WENT IN DEBT FOR FIRST PLOW

GOOD MACHINES SAVE LABOR AND
MAKE FARM WORK PROFITABLE

acres of sod per day, say you use it only thirty days in the year, and it lasts 15 years, then it had turned 1350 acres, and cost about $13.50, which was about one cent per acre. A stalk cutter will cut ten to twelve acres of stalks per day, and do a good job of it, and while it costs about $30.00, still you wouldn't try the job nowadays with a

hoe. I use three and four row stalk cutters, also stalk breaks thirty-two feet long. A self binder will handle from twelve to fifteen acres of grain in a day, and requires an outlay of about ten to fifteen cents per acre, still how much would it require in additional labor to handle the crop? With the single shovel, a man could do a fair piece of scratching, and cover about four acres per day, while with the common single row cultivator he can do a much better job and do eight acres, and with the modern two-row cultivator he can as

easily do fourteen to sixteen acres. I am telling you this to impress you with the fact that the cost of machinery doesn't amount to anything. The two-row cultivator will do better work, and cut the cost too, by lessening the amount of labor, both men and horses.

In 1847, I drove a bunch of cattle, about fifty head, to Chicago. I drove them across the prairie so they could feed as we traveled, and we would go to the edge of the timber to stay all night. As the settlers in those days, and as they have always done since, settled on the poorest ground, as they must be close to wood and water, as they were afraid they would freeze if they were out on the prairie, and when I could buy land I took the prairie and took my chance of freezing. We had to drive them about 200 miles, and, of course had to sell them to the butcher in the fall, who packed the meat and shipped it to the old country; that was the only time

PIONEERS SETTLED ON POOREST LAND NEAR WATER

HE BOUGHT PRAIRIE LAND—RISKING FREEZING

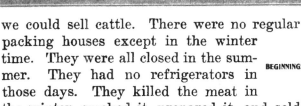

we could sell cattle. There were no regular packing houses except in the winter time. They were all closed in the summer. They had no refrigerators in those days. They killed the meat in the winter, smoked it, prepared it, and sold

BEGINNINGS OF THE PACKING INDUSTRY

it in the summer. They didn't know about putting up meat in cold storage. I was acquainted with Swift when he first commenced business, also Morris and Armour. Plankington and Armour were first in Milwaukee, then Armour came down to Chicago and started up alone.

The stockyards in Chicago were not much larger than the average loading and unloading yards of the small town of today, and it did not cover one-half an acre of ground. There was only one bridge across the Chicago river in those days, and that was at the foot of Lake street. The wild prairie extended up within a block or two of the court house. They butchered my cattle then about one and one-half miles from the court house, up the Chicago river. The Mayor about that time was "Long John" Wentworth. I bought a quarter section of land from him the same year and paid him $200. He was acting as agent for a man in New York. This land was located four and one-half miles south of Biggsville. There were no railroads running into Chicago at that time.

While on this trip to Chicago I saw the first practical reaper. It was made by McCormick. In 1848 I bought one. I think I paid $125 for it. This machine would cut a swath about five feet wide. As I remember, the grain fell on a platform and was raked off by another man with a fork or a rake, requiring two men to run the machine, and men followed and tied the bundles by hand with straw bands. This was a great improvement over the old cradle, but is not to

22

be compared at all with the modern self-binder.

The first reaper had a sickle a good deal like a saw, it was one solid bar with teeth cut in it. The whole machine was wood except a few parts, sickle, shafting, etc. The guards were made of iron and driven into a wood sickle bar. This machine, you know, took two men to operate it, one to drive the team, the other to rake off the grain. The man that operated the rake was a handy workman and got the best pay. It was pretty hard work, too. You see, he was in a sort of stooping position and had to lean away over to rake the wheat back in bundles so it could be bound. The rake was of peculiar construction, something of the style of the ordinary garden rake, and all wood, but instead of the rake bar being at right angles with the handle, it was more of a triangle shape, the end

Something Like His First Reaper.

of the left side being much farther from the handle than the end of the right side. This was so the wheat in being dragged around in a semi-circle would leave the straws as nearly straight as possible and bunched as it was shoved off from the platform. It took four horses to pull this machine, and they had something to do, too. You see, the construction was very crude indeed—didn't know what it was to have a babbitted or brass box like we get on the machines today. The reel was a mighty poor excuse.

In 1849, by the use of this McCormick machine I was able to carry on the harvest without whiskey the first time. In those days if you didn't have whiskey you couldn't get hands to harvest. I have always said that McCormick made it possible for me to do my harvesting without liquor. Here is a case where an improved farm implement helped me in two ways—to reduce the cost of harvesting and to enable me to take a stand in defense of temperance. If a man has the courage to stand by his convictions he will get along. What a ridiculous thing for people to say "can't." My! My! No one ever amounted to anything morally, mentally, physically or financially that could not say yes and no, so everybody could understand just what was meant. Few men realize what McCormick has done for the wheat grower, and the same is true of other inventors. We do not appreciate what John Deere has done with the steel plow to lessen labor for the farmer, in fact, made plowing a pleasure. If anybody used a wooden mouldboard they know what it is to stop every few rods and scrape the dirt off so it will shove the land over.

I was determined to run my business without liquor, and to be on the side of temperance and good citizenship. A few years

McCORMICK REAPER ABOLISHED LIQ-UOR ON HARVEST FIELD—PRACTICAL PROHIBITION

NO PLACE IN THE LANGUAGE FOR "CAN'T"

before this, Abraham Lincoln asked the question in one of his speeches, "Who shall be excused for not giving aid to checking the rum curse?" That part of Lincoln's address referred to is: "The demon of intemperance ever seems to have delighted in sucking the blood of genius and generosity. He seems to have gone forth, like the Egyptian angel of death, commissioned to slay, if not the first the fairest born of every family. Shall he not be arrested in his desolating career? In that arrest all can give aid that will, and who shall be excused that can and will not?"

I think Case, with his threshing machine was next in helping the farmer. Every inventor of farm machinery has lightened the labors of the farmer. Think how cheap you can buy these machines. I never begrudged the implement manufacturer the money I paid for labor-saving machines, but I have always been in the market, and am yet, for any machine that will save labor, or that will make the labor easier for the operators.

THRESHING MACHINE NEXT TO LIGHTEN FARMER'S LABOR

ALWAYS BOUGHT MACHINE IF IT DID GOOD WORK AND SAVED LABOR

I was married in 1850 to my first wife. Her maiden name was Sarah Thompson. She died in 1878.

We had three children by this marriage:

Nettie, who married Mr. J. F. Hanna, and is now living in Riverside, California.

John A. Rankin, now of Greely, Colorado, and engaged in Farming and Banking.

William F. Rankin, of Tarkio, Missouri, and engaged in Farming and Banking.

My second marriage was in the fall of 1879, to Elizabeth Phillips, who is still living.

We had one daughter by this marriage, Esther B.

When I married, in 1850, I had eighty acres of land and a few cattle. I had raised a crop of wheat on the land before I got a deed to it. All the money I had I invested in young steers. When I got married I had only $4.00 or $5.00 in cash. This I gave to the preacher—the last cent I had. We had to trade for everything. I could not get first-class flour without paying cash for it, so I had to buy second-class flour on credit. It was packed solid in the barrel and my wife scooped out a place in the flour in the top of the barrel, and in this improvised bowl made our bread. She had to make bread in this way from the 21st of March until cucumber time, when the old tinner brought the big tin dishpan, for which I had traded lumber that spring. Up to this time she washed her dishes in the stove kettle. We had a nice little three room house 16x24 feet, all made of native lumber. We bought the shingles that had been rafted down the Mississippi river from up north. Fine lumber was sold for $10.00 per

thousand—just as fine boards as you would want to look at—and common lumber or grub plank, for $5.50 per thousand feet. We made cribs of any kind of lumber, no matter how good it was. It was floated down the river on a raft and was very cheap. Even walnut lumber, which is being scraped up and shipped to Europe in such quantities now, from wherever they can find it only brought $10.00 per thousand then. In fact, most of our furniture was made from it, be- WALNUT LUMBER ONLY WORTH $10.00 THOUSAND THEN cause it was a nice straight grained wood and worked up easily by hand as that was the way all the furniture was made

Our trading points were at Oquawka, Illinois, and Burlington, Iowa, twelve miles from my farm to either place. There was a ferry boat at Burlington across the Mississippi river. We drove oxen and it would take a day and a night to drive to town and back.

At Burlington the houses were along the river. There were only a few of them then, but it afterwards got to be quite a fine city. The land on which it was located was a part of the Black Hawk purchase and just came onto the market about that time. Father had some brothers west of the Mississippi but he stayed on the east side and never went across. He was determined to stay among the religious people.

It was a common thing for people to raise crops for years on land without any title to it, and later on buy it if they could. I bought a quarter section of land for $125 for father. A man named Wal- BOUGHT A QUARTER SECTION OF LAND FOR $125 lace concluded he would fix up a quarter just east of us and join with father, and they would need no division fences. Wallace agreed that father should have part of the land when he bought it, say two or three years afterwards, when he would be able to make a payment on it. One day father was stacking oats for me and I was pitching. That was in the year 1852. Wallace said to father, "You can have that eighty acres of land for $450." About sixty acres were broken and all of it was fenced with rail fence. Father said to him, "I can't buy it, as I have no money." Well, I had gotten so I could "brush around" and get a little money then, as I was of the "twisting" kind anyway. Father didn't have as much twist as I had. because, with mother's help I had minded his business affairs for several years.

My mother was a business woman. I said I would buy this land and father said "You buy it and make the first payment and I'll take it." I bought the land for him and he rented it back to Wallace, father to get one-third of the crop. Lots of people thought it better to rent land in those days than to own it, but I couldn't see it that way.

Later in the fall of the year that I married I bought 320 acres of land. There was a quarter section east of the house for sale and I had about $50 in money. My brother-in-law also had about $50, so we went down to Quincy to buy this piece of land east of the house for me, and a piece north of the house for him. He couldn't get the north place, so he let me have his $50 and I bought the quarter section right east of me for $200 and paid $50 on it. Then I bought another quarter section just one mile north of us and paid

28

$50 on it. So in these two deals I got 320 acres of land and that made me a total of 400 acres. As I told you, my first home, where we first began housekeeping, was a little house, and it was on the first eighty acres of land I ever owned—the first time David Rankin's name was ever written on a warranty deed. This was in Henderson county, Illinois. We thought it a very good home, and I thought I was somewhat of a farmer then. I broke the land up and put it in wheat a year or two and that made me more money than I had ever had before. We would raise wheat two or three years on the land and then we changed to corn and fed it to cattle. I just kept on buying more and more land until I got to where I am now.

In 1853 McCormick's Improved Reaper and John Deere's steel plow gave me inspira-

Mr. Rankin's
First Cultivator.

tion to look further into other kinds of machinery and I conceived the idea to put together two of my double shovel plows so as to make a plow that would plow on both sides of the row. I had the neighborhood blacksmith make the

29

iron pieces for me and I took a four by six oak and made an axle to fit the front wheels of my wagon, bolted a tongue to the center, then made a connection of the plow beams to the axle by means of large round iron, one inch or an inch and-a-half eye bolts and rings. I took a board and tied it across the handles of the two plows and with this equipment I did just as much work as a hired man and I had been doing, and I firmly believe that this was the first straddle row cultivator ever made, which afterwards came into general use. It was only a few years after this that manufacturers who had been making the single and double shovel plows put on the market what were then known as the strad-

FARMER TODAY HAS EVEN GREATER OPPORTUNITY THAN THEN

dle-row cultivator, and when I compare the crude idea I made with the neatly painted and ornamented cultivators of today, I feel like saying that there is certainly just as great, if not greater opportunity for the farmer of today than then. And right here I want to tell you that what is true of big manufacturers, packers and railroads is equally true of the farmers—yes, more so. To make a profit he must reduce cost of production. I saw this long ago, and when I saved a hand's wages by the use of my new cultivator I felt pretty good—that was making money for me.

You see we farmers must not only keep eternally at reducing cost of production but plan a way to get the most out of our product —use your head as well as your hands, for it is the little savings that make up the profit at the end of the year. It takes sharpening of wits all the time. Remember, we farmers must figure for ourselves—the other fellow looks out for his own interests.

About 1854 or 1855, Nelson Morris was buying dead hogs at the Sherman yards— hogs that had been killed in shipping. Dead hogs sold as well, or higher in proportion than live ones in those days. The Sherman yards were located about four miles south of the court house, near the Douglas Monument, as well as I can remember. There were two or three other selling yards around Chicago— one at Fort Wayne, just across the Chicago river, near where the Burlington railroad goes into Chicago, and the others were located about at Twenty-second street. These yards were the beginning of Chicago's stockyards. No one ever dreamed that it was the beginning of the world's greatest stock market.

BOUGHT AND SOLD THOUSANDS OF HOGS WITHOUT STOCK SCALES— WEIGHED WITH BREECHING

I bought and sold hogs and shipped them by the thousand to New York before I had a stock scale. In order to get the weight of the hogs, a device was made which we called a breeching. The hog was lifted off of the ground by two or three men and weighed by a pair of old "steel-yards," which was a sort of hanging balance. Later on the common portable platform scale came into use and a little box or crate was made that just held one hog and

31

they were driven across or through this crate and weighed singly. The first big stock scale that I ever owned was built right on my farm by a blacksmith. We bought a few of the parts from an agent who came along who was called a scale builder. Cattle were sold by the head, as there was no means of weighing.

As an illustration, a neighbor sold a drove of cattle to be fed and to be delivered in the spring. They picked out an average steer, and then when dressed to be weighed, the weight of this steer to decide the weight of the drove.

From 1852 until about 1861 I paid from fifteen to eighteen per cent for borrowed money, but that gave me a chance to

PAID 18 PER CENT FOR MONEY—AND MADE IT PAY

AND THIS WHEN CORN BROUGHT 8 CENTS A BUSHEL DELIVERED

buy land and it was a great accommodation to get money then at any price. During the panic of '57 nearly every bank in the country broke up. You could buy corn at any price if you had the cash—as low as eight and ten cents per bushel. They would even haul it ten miles with oxen and deliver it at that price. I built a barn and filled up the cribs with corn, which I held for two or three years, then sold it to the Oquawka still right in the crib for eighty cents per bushel. I didn't begin to make much money until 1865. I had acquired property, for I always invested my profits in land, borrowed money to operate

"KEEP YOUR MONEY IN THE FARM—IT'S GOOD BUSINESS"

on, and I still consider that a business proposition. Keep your own money in the farm. After that year the land I had been buying and paying such high interest on for borrowed money went right up. It was only a short time before this I saw a man pay $260 in greenbacks for $100 in gold. During

32

the war greenbacks were greatly depreciated. Fifteen years before this I had been borrowing a great deal of money from a Mr. Moir and another man by the name of Edwards. They each loaned me a great deal of money, and while I paid them a big rate of interest, it was a great accommodation and I could not have accumulated so much if it had not been for the confidence these men had in me and furnishing me money. My wife was against my buying so much land and her folks were all against it too, but they once loaned me $1,100 to buy cattle. I was working like a Turk then. They argued that I had no business buying so much land. They had money to loan at six per cent, while I was paying eighteen per cent wherever I could get it. Finally, in three or four years, her brother said to me one day: "David, here's some money. You had just as well have it as anybody," so then I borrowed from them.

PAID 18 PER CENT FOR MONEY

A good many years after this time I went to see Mr. Moir, who was sick, and I told him "I have always come to borrow money of you before, but this time I have come to visit you." "Yes," said he, "We have had fifty years of business together. We might have had fifty fights, but we didn't have one." He was a fine man.

It was about 1865 that I bought cattle at $1.50 to $1.75 a hundred in Chicago, took them down to Paxton, put them on the prairie, fed them corn and fattened them, and sold them in New York for $6.00 to $6.50 a hundred. I invested the money, and some more that I had accumulated the same way in land east of Pax-

CATTLE BOUGHT AT $1.50 SOLD AT S6.50 A HUNDRED

33

ton, buying about 5,000 acres at from $6.25 to $7.00 per acre. The town of Rankin was established and is now located on this land. If I had never sold any land, I would be richer than a king. On this very land we raised broom corn and sold it as high as $320 a ton in Chicago. I never saw such heavy stuff as it was in my life. The people around there had been losing by farming, and when they saw me start in the broom corn business, they said: "That fool will break up." But instead of breaking up I made $200,000.00 out of it. At that time I could have bought land north of Bloomington, and any quantity of it from $8.00 to $10.00 an acre. From that time on I began buying land, I always tried to buy in large bodies, and it has paid me big.

RAISED BROOM CORN AND SOLD IT AT $320.00 A TON, MAKING $200,000

This was about the time I put up my first windmill, and it was the first mill in western Illinois, at least that I knew of. I

bought the mill in Batavia from the United States Wind Engine and Pump Company, and I think they called the mill the HALLADAY. People were very skeptical in those days about any new invention, and several of my neighbors said that I had gone crazy when they heard about my

BOUGHT THE FIRST WINDMILL IN WESTERN ILLINOIS AND WAS CALLED CRAZY

having ordered a windmill. In fact, I became the laughing stock of the country until the mill was put up and in actual use. One man said, "Dave, the blamed fool, thinks he can pump

Not the First Windmill, but one of 75 Required to Pump Fresh Water for 35,000 Fattening Cattle and Hogs, Horses and Mules.

water with the wind. Now, what do you suppose he'll try next?" This first windmill was as good a one as I ever owned, and it saved me a world of work, always ALWAYS HAD FRESH WATER FOR STOCK had the water ready for the stock. As my possessions increased I bought four or five of these HALLADAY wildmills.

I built my mansion as I thought of it, right on the very spot where our first little house stood. This was in 1865, I now had 4000 acres of land and was getting along fine. This is where three of my children were born, and for that matter, practically raised. We had only public schools for them, and I was glad we had such schools. I have always been a great believer in the public school system of our country.

When my children were in the public schools, the average wages for school teachers was about $40.00, but being interested in the education of my own children, and the neighbors', I got our people to pay higher

His Mansion in Illinois.

wages. We paid $25.00 to $35.00 more per month to the teacher in our school than any in the country. We wanted the best instruction we could get for our children, and this very school, on account of having such an efficient teacher, fitted its pupils for the Freshman class of the college. You know, in those days six months was the school year, as we could not spare our boys off of

WENT TO EUROPE TO BUY HORSES the farm any longer than that. In the summer time they had to be in the field.

About this time I went to Europe to buy some horses. I bought some fine mares in Liverpool as I was coming back. Two men were with me. We went from New York to Queenstown, Ireland. We went through England, Ireland and Scotland. From England we went to Belgium, crossing the channel, then up into France. We don't appreciate the kind of land we have in this country. I didn't until after I made a trip across the water. In England it is just AFTER VISITING EUROPE THANKFUL HE WAS BORN IN AMERICA like plowing rock, though there is some fine land there. Most of the land in France is pretty good, but does not compare with American soil. And the plows were ridiculous things. They didn't plow as we do here. They have fine wagon roads. You can't walk on the railroad there, and when you are crossing they watch you like you had no sense. My trip made me think lots more of the United States, and I was thankful I was born in America. I was more than thankful that I was born in the West, too. This trip was a profitable one, as a matter of education to me. This was before I moved out to Missouri. I shipped three hundred cattle to Liverpool at one time, but after paying the expenses on the shipment, I didn't make any more money out of them than I would if

I had sold them in Chicago, taking into consideration the trouble and the risk.

I got into politics in Illinois before I knew it—never dreamed of such a thing—and I guess I was more surprised than any one else when I learned that I had been nominated for the legislature. I didn't even attend the convention. The facts are at that time everything was against the Republicans, and none of us had any hopes of being elected, and I never would have been had it not been for my Democratic friends who got out and worked for me. One of them used as his argument in electioneering for me, "Rankin gave me the best advice of anybody during the war. He said, 'Keep your clothes on. We are all in danger.'" I served three times in the legislature, from 1874 to 1880.

About the time I was elected there was
SERVED IN THE ILLINOIS LEGISLATURE —INVESTIGATED ¦PRISON CONDITIONS AT JOLIET
a great deal of complaint about the prison officials and some of their actions, and the people were complaining a great deal. A special commission was appointed by the governor to investigate the matter and I was one of the board. A trial was held at Joliet and we were the judges. Lawyers were employed for each side and the trial lasted a week or so. The prison officials were a regular set of rascals, and a good many of the people in Joliet seemed to know it. Some of the members of the legislature wore plug hats and put on a lot of style, and the prison officials treated them mighty fine. They gave me the Governor's room and were mighty nice to me. I imagined they were afraid they couldn't handle me. They had about $30,000 prison profits with which they had started a bank down at Carlinville. They

sold suits of clothes to the state for big prices, some of which were from a shipment of clothes that was sunk in the Mississippi river. They were water damaged goods, but they put them in for full price. They fitted the prisoners out with the poorest kind of clothes, for which they charged $10.00 a suit. I went up town and bought a better suit for $4.50 and hung it up in the Assembly Hall to compare with the ones they were furnishing for $10.00. This raised a terrible hubbub. The commissioners, or prison officials, looked pretty sick. I thought I had the other members of the committee with me but they deserted. They argued with me that "these are our people (meaning our party), and we should take care of them." I said, "I don't know anybody, Republicans or Democrats, in this matter. I am not working for any party, but for the State of Illinois."

PRISON OFFICIALS STARTED A BANK WITH PRISON PROFITS

DIDN'T KNOW REPUBLICANS OR DEMOCRATS IN INVESTIGATION

The following editorial from one of the leading papers of that time indicates the feeling of my constituents:

"The committee appointed to investigate the alleged frauds committed by the Penitentiary commissioners are proceeding with their work as fast as possible, but have not as yet made any report. Hon. David Rankin was appointed one of the committee, and it seems that he is making it hot for some of the gentlemen concerned in it. We clip from the Inter-Ocean of Saturday, the following extract from its telegraphic dispatches:"

"After adjourning today, Mr. Rankin, of the Penitentiary Committee, was attacked by J. L. Ward, counsel for the Commissioners, and Rowett. They accused him of undue diligence in the investigation and took occasion to severely abuse him for his course. Mr. Rankin explained that he knew neither friend nor foe in the matter, but he was TELEGRAPHIC DISPATCH TO INTER-OCEAN determined to go to the bottom of the investigation and to perform his whole duty without fear or favor. A sub-committee of Messrs. Barclay, Rankin and Easly will go to Joliet next week to close the investigation.''

''We are glad to see that Mr. Rankin takes hold of the matter in earnest, and the fact that the counsel for the commissioners made such an attack upon him shows that he is probing the matter to the bottom, and if there is anything wrong in the management of the penitentiary, that he will bring it to light.''

I would not sign any whitewash or false statement about the matter, so I made a minority report of my findings of the investigation. When the Governor saw my report he said it looked like the report of an honest man and accepted it. This was Governor Beveridge. I met him again in California about forty years afterwards. I told his wife that people were calling me Governor Beveridge and she said: ''I thought you were the Governor myself when I saw you coming.''

One of the members of the committee WOULDN'T SIGN ANY WHITEWASH said to me about five years afterwards: ''Rankin, you were right, and we were wrong in that prison matter.''

I tell you I was glad I had got started farming. I did not have any such things to tempt me in my business, and many times since I have thought about it.

You see, farming is creative. You make

the wealth by the "toil in the soil," and it belongs to you because you make it.

The last time I was elected I said to my friends, "You must not nominate me." I felt that I couldn't go to the legislature again,

Working in the Soil.

as I couldn't afford it. It cost me $25,000 to go if it cost me a cent. I was beginning to buy land in northwest Missouri and southwest Iowa for almost nothing, as we say "for a song," and was making piles of money on it. I was buying good land for from $5.00 to $10.00 an acre.

Yes, I have attended all of the World's Fairs held in this country. I remember well the Centennial at Philadelphia. It was the greatest show I had even seen. There were exhibits from all the countries then friendly with our nation, and some odd sights indeed. Of course, I was interested in the way farming was done in other countries and spent most of my time in the agricultural exhibits. I think this was the first time England and other countries realized what a wonderful country we had, especially our farming interests, which were well exhibited. It showed to me what our resources were, and I became convinced that the whole world must look to

ATTENDED ALL FAIRS AND BELIEVES THEM GREAT EDUCATORS—BUT WENT TO NO SHOWS

CENTENNIAL AT PHILADELPHIA GREAT

us for bread and meat, and that has helped me in my farming.

I never went to shows. Maybe it was because I didn't have any money. At any rate, I never attended many shows, except these World's Fairs, and, of course, the State Fairs. I am a strong believer in the country folks exhibiting their products. It is the thing for them to do. These different state corn shows where the farmers contest in exhibiting the best corn grown affords great education. I have attended several of them and have gained much information each time.

The World's Fair at Chicago was the next great show and it so far outclassed the Centennial that I said then that it was

WORLD'S COLUMBIAN EXPOSITION AT CHICAGO GREATER LOUISIANA PURCHASE EXPOSITION AT ST. LOUIS GREATEST

the greatest show the world ever saw. It was so immensly greater than the Centennial that the Centennial was only a county fair in comparison. It was, however, only a collection of facts that existed all over the world and was the one thing that marked the pace of development which we were making. I knew I had been making great strides for a common farmer and I was awfully glad to find that every other line of industry had made equal progress, if not greater.

It was the common comment at that time, during the World's Fair at Chicago, that the world's fairs had reached their zenith, but just see how little people knew what they were talking about, for in only ten years all past efforts were totally eclipsed.

The World's Fair at St. Louis was the greatest show. I always said that it was the United States entertaining the World in Missouri.

Yes, that field scene was made out of corn and grass, and really reproduced my largest farm. That 6,000 acre corn field was a sight for some, and others, I understand,

One of Rankins Fields Reproduced at World's Fair.

did not believe it was true. One fellow from Australia came up to Tarkio to see if it really existed. Then there was a man from South Africa became interested and said he hoped to see such fields in his country some time.

The state of Missouri was looking for such things to show—as you know it is called the "show you" state, and say, H. J. Waters, who is dean of the College at Columbia, and was at that time, is all and always for Missouri. He was up here and went out on the farms several times. The state don't always appreciate such men as this I am sure. Of course the state expended a lot of money to exhibit such a picture. It gave me some notoriety, but gave the state far more. Yes indeed, there were forty-two two-row cultivators in that picture, and that was only one-third of the number I had at work that

42 TWO-ROW CULTIVATORS AT WORK day. Mr. Waters said when they were all lined up, "Well, well, that looks like cavalry mobilizing"—and I guess it did.

I raise a great many hogs, and have done fairly well with them. Where you feed cattle, hogs are a great necessity to gather up the waste. We have about 25,000 hogs each year.

Just a word about corn. I have been asked a great many times about my methods of planting corn. Of course, I aim to get my ground in the very best condition and the corn evenly planted. I plow some of the ground, but use the lister mostly, and plant with the planter after the lister.

I plant several varieties of corn. I am always experimenting, and am always in the market for the very choicest kinds. I

CORN THAT HAS A GRANDFATHER IS THE BEST SEED CORN do not try to breed seed corn for my own use, but depend on the breeder of the different varieties which are best adapted for our locality.

Each year I use from 4000 to 6000 bushels of corn for seed, and as I have stated, regard this as one of the essential things for a good corn crop.

To raise a good corn crop I follow this method:

Keep my ground rich. Feed cattle and hogs on it, and use the manure spreader.

Plow deep and turn the ground completely over—leave no skips.

Have the ground well pulverized before planting, either by harrowing or disking.

Plant the corn at a uniform depth. Early planting, shallow—late planting deeper.

Harrow thoroughly before the corn comes up, once at least, but twice is better.

Cultivate as soon as possible, and as often and thoroughly as you can. Never less than four or five times. Corn should be gone over with cultivator at least once a week. Stirring the ground, conserves the moisture.

During the month of August go through the fields and pull every cockle burr, button weed and all obnoxious weeds.

Improved Machinery Makes Good Corn Shows.

If the lister is used—I disk the land once or twice before going in with the listers, so the weeds get a good start before planting, is the idea.

Cultivate weeds before planting corn, so you can kill them while cultivating the corn to make it grow.

Then when I raise four, five, or more crops, just as the land will stand, I sow my corn field down to clover and timothy, and begin to pasture and feed on the land three to five years, and get good rich ROTATES CROP TO KEEP LAND UP soil. Then again plow up the sod, and raise corn again for a term of years.

Away back, when I first began buying land in Illinois I had an eye to business with regard to corn growing. I felt sure there was a great future to corn and I was determined to own only such land as I could grow corn or clover on at will. I have never changed my mind. I will admit, however, that the corn crop has become more important than I

expected, i. e., it has found avenues of trade that I did not dream of. Take for instance the cereal products of this country. I understand that about 100 different kinds of food products are made from corn. A great number of the breakfast foods are made from corn, and they're good, too. Nearly everybody used to think that corn was only good for cattle, horses, hogs and sheep, but with all the aristocracy of the American people they find it is about as good a thing as they can eat.

I saw, years ago, yes, when I was a boy, that the time would never come when corn would not be in demand, as it took corn to make the best beef and pork, and as I said made up my mind that as for me I was going to be a corn farmer.

SAW YEARS AGO THAT CORN WAS TO BE WORLD'S MOST IMPORTANT CROP

I saw this too, that not until agricultural science marks time with manufacturing science would we realize the possibilities of the farmer.

I did not know at that time the corn growing area was as limited as it is. We will never see cheap corn again in this country. That is not all—there is no way to make more acres to grow corn. What we farmers have got to do is to figure how to get more corn per acre, and yet not increase the expense of producing it. Adopt tactics of big manufacturing plants, railroads, etc. They don't stop for cost of equipment if greater results may be reached or expense reduced. Intensive and extensive farming must go PROBLEM IS TO RAISE MORE CORN PER ACRE AND DECREASE COST OF DOING IT hand in hand to make corn growing successful. You have to have machinery with which you can do twice as much work as we used to to make it pay, for the land is getting higher all the time, and it is going to get higher. This land is cheap yet. Then we have got to practice book farming a whole lot —work to increase our fertilizer, and then utilize it to the best possible advantage. The manure spreader must be used freely. I regard it one of the machines that actually grinds out money for me. Lots of machines I have bought save me money, but I believe the manure spreader actually makes me money.

The way I keep my corn land in such a high state of fertility is by keeping a lot of it in tame grass, using it for feed lots or

pastures as some call them, and then where there are weak places that require an extra amount of fertilizer I bring my manure spreader into use. It pays to use it, and it will pay every farmer to have a spreader and then use it. Hunt up these weak places. There is no land but what has them, unless it is rich

A Farm Machine That Will Coin Money.

valley land. I have some of this of course, but I am talking about my land in general.

"Seed corn" is one of the important features of corn growing, and too much encouragement can not be given to the man who devotes his time to the breeding of seed corn. Farming in a large way as I do, I have never been able to give this part of corn-growing the attention it should receive. Good seed corn is cheap at five times the price of ordinary market corn.

Agricultural schools for the boys deserve support. I advise the boys to study agriculture, and have often said that we farmers should see to it that the boys are educated to farm and to like the farm.

My! My! Why anyone wants to leave and go to the city I can't see. I like to be on the farm all the time, as close to nature as possible.

I crib the corn on the different

48

farms where it is raised. My farms vary in size from 700 to 8000 acres each. My feed lots are a great surprise to some of my visi-

tors. The smallest I have covers 160 acres. I have others of 240 to 320 acres, and some as high as 640 acres. These we call feed lots. My largest farm contains 8,000 acres, 6,000 acres of which I put in corn and the balance is in grass, feed yards, etc. All my land is fenced hog tight. Some of the boys have figured out that it makes 420 miles of fencing. I have had some very large average yields of corn, and of course some very light ones, depending a good deal on the season. I had one field of 50 acres which averaged 118 bushels to the acre. I think our corn would average, one

FEED LOTS FROM 160 TO 640 ACRES

FOUR HUNDRED MILES OF HOG TIGHT FENCE ON FARMS

FIFTY ACRES OF CORN AVERAGED 118 BUSHELS AN ACRE

David Rankin Ready for an Inspection Trip.

49

year with another, about 40 to 60 bushels to the acre. Our largest acreage was **EIGHTEEN THOUSAND ACRES IN CORN EACH YEAR** planted in 1906, about 19,000 acres, in 1908 about 18,000 acres. I have one

corn crib which everybody calls the big crib which holds 25,196 bushels of corn. Some of my corn is raised on shares, in which case I usually turn over a body of land **25,000 BUSHELS OF CORN IN ONE CRIB** to a good reliable farmer who farms it on shares. I furnish the money for stock, etc., to run the farm, he pays interest on half of the money furnished. Last year two of my foremen in this way handled 4,000 acres apiece, and they cleared about $12,000

Another of the 75 Windmills at Work.

each, which is not so very bad. I also furnish the land to others and let them raise corn for me at so much a bushel for all FOREMEN CLEAR $12,000 A YEAR ON SHARES raised.

I contend that much of my success is due to good judgment in selecting assistants, my foremen, as I call them—partners in reality. And well they are deserving of the title. A good man is cheap at most any price, and a shiftless, careless man is dear if he works for nothing.

I am often asked how many acres of land I have, and it is seldom that I can tell exactly, which may appear strange to my friends and visitors, but you see I have been buying land all the time. I rarely ever sell any. Sometimes I buy in small lots and BUY LAND IN EITHER SMALL OR LARGE AMOUNTS sometimes I buy several thousand acres at a single purchase. I have just bought some more land.

Two More Cribs That Hold 10,00 Bushels Each.

I have a bookkeeper in my office who looks after all of these records of my transactions and I never bother by mind very much with how much I have, either in land or other things. I try to see that everything is moving along in good shape, that all the farms are well cultivated and kept, that all the foremen and renters and men are well fixed and cared for, that all farms are kept supplied with plenty of livestock, and that there is always plenty of good grain on hand for feeding, both for the work horses and also for the fattening stock. As I say, I do not worry much about keeping track of what I have.

A Home Scene—Shredding Corn.

I have a great many advantages now which I did not have in early days, both for marketing fattened stock and in purchasing feeders. At first I had to ship stock to the New York market. Later we got a good market at Chicago, and now I have three or four good markets right at home on the Missouri river, one at Kansas City, one at St. Joseph, and one at Omaha; and these are also good markets to buy feeders to replenish the fattening yards.

GOOD LIVESTOCK MARKET NOW NEARER HOME

This convenience of markets is a great advantage, particularly as it enables us to get our fattened product to market with as little shrinkage, and this is of equal advantage to the small feeder, and the heavier one.

I used to buy a good many feeders and in quite large quantities from the ranches direct in Texas, Colorado and in other places, but in late years I have found that we can do best, or just about as well, by buying at home in these great markets of ours.

When I get short of feeders I can go to one of the markets, pick up five, ten, fifteen or twenty cars of them and have them at my place in a few hours, and save all the worry and risk of the long shipments. When I shipped direct from the ranches I usually bought them in large quantities—one time as many as 240 cars. The freight bill of the railroad company on this shipment was about $12,000.

I am also often asked how much my farms and stock are worth, and I cannot often tell them within a quarter of a million dollars.

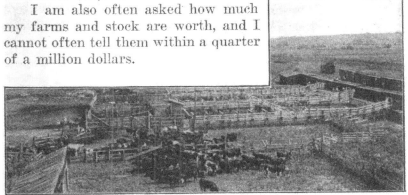

Receiving Feeders

To keep me up with the times I had to make Double Row Listers and other implements of big capacity. This took lots of planning. I encountered plenty of discouragement and could not get any manufacturer to build these new ideas without lots of persuasion and pay. Work or no work, I told them that they were to be my property. They worked.

Yes, these double listers looked odd, and were clumsy, ill proportioned machines, but they did the business. One man could do the work of two, and do it just as good—better.

Well, I guess they have been adopted by other farmers. You look around and you will see several of the plow companies are making them. No, I never took out a patent. The plow was what I wanted, not patents.

Of course many improvements had to be made from time to time but the principles were right. I am no mechanic, but I could see my needs and that made me study for a way out, and I have been successful in making them by the help of skilled workmen who would build what I planned.

I had three and four-row stalk cutters made also; big harrows and all such things that require six to twelve mules. In-

HAD SPECIAL MACHINERY MADE TO SUIT ME

creased capacity is what I am after all the time, provided the work is done as good.

I have said before that I was the first to buy new improved farm implements whether the old ones were worn out or not. And of course was the first to get the profits on the improved machine in our locality.

If the new machine had greater capacity and did good work, that was what I wanted.

This is the only way. Run the farm

TWO-ROW MACHINERY SAVES $20,000 A YEAR

like any great enterprise and you are sure to succeed. Just take a moment and figure. I grow about 18,000 acres of corn a year, and these double-row machines save me $20,000 each year.

Now, the cost of two one-row riding cultivators is equal, or more than one two-row machine, so you see I make big money by using the two-row cultivator. I raise

NOW FARMERS MUST PLANT AND CUL-TIVATE TWO ROWS AT ONCE

good corn too, and weeds are about as scarce in my corn fields as in my neighbor's fields. We all have more weeds than we ought to have.

I don't know any better way to make

Seeing That the Fields Are Well Cultivated—24 Two-Row Cultivators at Work.

money than to save it. The two-row cultivator will save money. I use large mowers, large binders, gang plows, and in fact everything I get of as great capacity as possible so as to save labor, which is scarce and expensive.

SAVES HALF OF CULTIVATING BILL BY USING TWO-ROW CULTIVATOR

After I have grown these big crops of corn, get my hay in the barns and stacks, and my corn in the cribs, then I am ready with a large number of stock cattle and hogs to convert it into market shape. I usually raise about one million bushels of corn and I buy a large amount more to fill out on.

GROWS FROM ONE MILLION BUSHELS TO ONE AND ONE-HALF MILLIONS CORN CROP EACH YEAR

BUYS A GREAT MANY BUSHELS MORE CORN--ALL FED ON LAND TO KEEP LAND FERTILE

After I get my crops all harvested and a good bunch of steers on each farm, I feel contented, as the mills are grinding. I have about 25,000 head of hogs each year and we usually figure about three hogs to the steer, some years more and some years less. I keep about one thousand head of work horses and mules, and I aim to keep good ones. I have a few prime teams of mules which I have bought in the past year, the average are worth from $150 to

I DON'T KNOW ANY BETTER WAY TO MAKE MONEY THAN TO SAVE IT

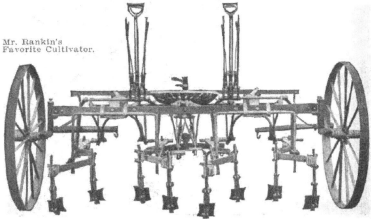

Mr. Rankin's Favorite Cultivator.

$225 each. I keep plenty of them, and every one as fat as butter, and when they are in the harness they are always able and willing to do a good honest day's work.

From first to last on all the farms I have the reputation of having good substan-

tial equipment, but with no attention paid to style or show. There is only one place in my business that I care for a showing, and that is when we balance the books at the end of the year. To carry on the busi- ness I have worked out a system adapt- ed to my farm operations which fits my requirements. I have an accurate record of all the different transactions. The farms are known by numbers and each is under the supervision of a competent foreman, with whom I am in direct communication by tele- phone at all times. Each foreman is equipped with a full set of blank reports, requisitions, etc., which facilitates the handling of my busi- ness, so that a few moments of clerical work by each foreman each day keep the records in my office in a complete and intelligent shape. My office, by the way, is a sort of a joke with my friends. It is only about 12x14 feet and usually well supplied with seed corn, repairs, harness, or some other farm paraphernalia. I have a fire-proof vault which is about as large as the office for keep-

MADE HIS OWN BOOK-KEEPING SYS- TEM—ONLY SHOW HE CARES FOR IS AT BALANCING OF BOOKS

ing my records. Our bank is in front of the office and my private secretary and book-keeper is equally expert with the pen, and the

Four Cassiday High-lift Gang Plows and 24 Mules Changing Meadow to Corn Field

saddle-horse, and he can always be found at the desk unless we are receiving or shipping a large bunch of stock; then he is in the saddle.

I pay all the men once a month. I have always made it a rule to pay my men good, fair wages, give them good board, and expect good, honest work in return. We have about 250 on an average. Some of my men have been with me a

ALWAYS PROFITABLE TO PROVIDE FARM LABOR WITH GOOD HOMES

GOOD WAGES TO GOOD MEN AND THEY WILL TREAT YOU RIGHT

Stacking Clover.

great many years, so long that they seem like part of the family.

I have had some very bright young men in my office who are now filling responsible places in banks and other lines of business. They seem to me like part of my family indeed. Of course, when I could help them get a better place I was glad to do it.

My inventory made September 1, 1908, showed a total valuation of $3,237,490.61, which, of course has greatly appreciated since that time, because land is going up very fast. The great bulk of this inventory is vested in rich farm land. MADE THREE AND A QUARTER MILLION DOLLARS FARMING

Part of the 1,000 Work Mules Ready For Work.

The remainder in live stock, grain and farming implements, and interests in commercial enterprises.

I have never indulged much in speculation. The greater part of my possessions has come by buying land, improving it, and from thorough and persistent farming. Of course, I have invested in large bunches of cattle when I thought the cattle were low, and put them in good market shape, holding them for a better market. I regard this simply as a business proposition, MONEY MADE ONLY IN LEGITIMATE BUSINESS and a part of modern farming, the same as a merchant would buy any class of goods for his shelves, which he would need for future

Filling Up Bed of Old River That Has Been Straightened.

demand, especially when he felt that the market was going to have a strong advance.

I have been asked why I always feed all my corn and I always say—first, I find it profitable to feed it, because in that way I can get full value out of it, and second-ly, I also gain an immense amount of fertilizer, and then to haul my corn to the railroad to ship would be a big job.

A SUCCESSFUL FARMERS' COMMAND-MENT—"THOU SHALT NOT SELL CORN"

And, further, I do not believe in selling raw material. You see, I run my farming business something on the plan of the manufacturing industries of the country. I want to sell the finished product, and can do so only by feeding all I raise to stock. If by doing so, I gain only an average of $1.00 a head for the cattle and hogs I feed, you see it pays me. But, of course, I expect to make more than that.

I would recommend to every farmer to feed his crops rather then haul the grain off the place. My observation is that a great many farmers do not carry out their work as far as they can. They sell too much raw material and not enough finished product. It is true, there are years that the return from a crop might be greater, but year in and year out, it will pay you to feed all you raise.

SELLS 35,000 HEAD FAT STOCK EACH YEAR · BUT NO CORN OR HAY

FEED THE CROPS ON FARM AND SHIP THE FINISHED PRODUCT

You must have a fixed way to do things —system, I suppose it would be called—if you ever expect to amount to anything.

What would you think of a carpenter that would come to build a house for you without a square or level? Don't you lose sight of the fact that a farmer, of all business men, must have fixed methods and cut to the line every way to get the most out of everything.

THE SECRET OF SUCCESSFUL FARMING—BY ONE WHO HAS SUCCEEDED

There are very few merchants, and equally as few manufacturing concerns, who do not have years that their profits are practically nothing, sometimes a loss, but at the end of a term of years the most of them have made a gain. I contend that farming requires closer figuring and more attention than any

One Machine Used (using 20 mules) to Make Rolling Land Out of Flat Bottoms.

other kind of business. You will also find that there are few, if any, successful mer-

Another Machine Used in the Same Work.

chants or manufacturers who do not take advantage of every modern method of reducing their cost of handling their product. It is essential for the farmer to keep abreast of the times with the modern methods and equipment, as all he has to deal with is raw material, and the cost of his product is principally labor.

And if he can save just a little here and a little there in the labor bill, he will find this will swell his profits just that much. Say, what I save in labor is not an item to be overlooked. You may make money, but unless you save it, at the end of the year you are no better off than when you started in.

MUST SAVE IN LABOR—MUST CALCULATE EXPENSES

Let me tell you, the farmer, as a rule, does not calculate cost enough or try to reduce the expense bill as he should.

I never stayed all night in our home town while my boys were young. I wanted to impress on their minds the importance of being

at home every night and ready for work early
in the morning. Sometimes it was a hardship
after reaching the railroad station, to
drive or to walk out four and one-half
miles to my home rather than go to the
hotel and wait until morning. However, you
see it did not shorten my days. That is no-
ticeable at any rate.

TO SELL CORN MAKES POOR, TO SELL
FAT STOCK MAKES RICH

TRIED TO BE AT HOME EVERY NIGHT

I feel well paid for the extra effort. I
tell you too much care cannot be given to boys
while they are young, and to get fixed habits
requires much thought, patience and consideration on the part of their parents; but just
you get a boy to see the proper course for him
to pursue and he is easily handled. To bed
early every night and up early every morning

David Rankin's Present Home.

is a good rule and your boys will enjoy farm life and naturally form a liking for the work. When they do any commendable thing always

Using Corn Harvesters For Cutting Corn.

show your appreciation. Tell them that's well done, or when good judgment has been exercised, say so.

I always talked to my boys as partners, counseled with them, and got many good ideas, too. Every farmer should talk

ALWAYS COUNSELED WITH MY BOYS MADE THEM MY PARTNERS

over and plan his work ahead of time with his boys. Teach them the business end of farming along with the way to plant and harvest. Explain the why of it, etc.

Shredding Corn Fodder That Has Been Cut Up.

How can you expect a boy to get the correct ideas of your busines if you don't talk it over with him and explain why you sell this bunch of cattle and hold another. Why you plow at a certain time, this part of the land and not that. Why you haul out manure and scatter it thin over the ground, and why some spots require it in preference to others. Always keep in mind that the boy must learn many things that seem very simple to you, and never lose sight of the fact that farming is a business, and that many years training is necessary for success.

IT PAYS TO EXPLAIN THINGS TO THE BOYS. THEY MUST LEARN

Certainly I'd have them work in the field—everywhere—how could they learn otherwise?

My boys had to work hard, and my girls, too. After my sons were grown men, one of them said to me one day: "I used to think you were awfully hard on us boys, but I see now you were right." I always depended on my boys, and they knew that I did. I believe it helps them to develop decision and not be dependent on any one's opinion.

MY BOYS AND GIRLS WORKED HARD TOO—IT WAS BEST FOR THEM

If you don't have a crop of good boys and girls you haven't anything.

I always allowed my boys to draw checks on my bank account, and expected them to show just where the money was used, etc. Even when they were away at school they used what money they needed, just drew a

Getting Ready For Their Turn.

check on my bank account. I tell you this is a test on a boy, to be away from home and have free use of money. It will show the business side of him quick. No! No! that is not the way I was raised. Father had no bank account, mighty few did—but we are progressing. I am glad of it. Indeed I am, and I am glad to see farmers getting anything and everything to make life more worth living—telephone, rural route, autos, etc.—all help the man, and make the country richer, too.

FATHER HAD NO BANK ACCOUNT

Another Rankin Farm Home.

That commission appointed by President Roosevelt was a move in the right direction, and I was glad to see that he took so much interest in the farmers. He ought to, and I guess everybody will take more interest in the farmer each year; and more than all, he should take interest in himself. I think that the report, suggestions, etc., made by the commission satisfied the president and demonstrated clearly that he had made no mistake in his selection.

Now, it's no trouble for a farmer to have all the luxuries of the day, have his home modern and up to date, and he ought to do it, too—have all the conveniences of a city home if he will just attend to his business and keep eternally at it and be abreast of the times with modern machinery, and not wait until his implements are completely worn out before getting new ones of the latest up-to-date type. Say, an old plow that is rickety and out of fix will soon cost in loss of time the price of a new one—this is true of every kind of implement, and nothing will do more to discourage your boys than to give them no account tools to work with.

Get the best and latest implements, they are the cheapest in the end. Anybody that ever used wood mouldboard plows understands what I mean.

He must also plan his work ahead and take advantage of conditions. What would you think of me if I started to market expecting to bring home a load of seed wheat or clover, and after I got there and had begun to load up, find that my team and wagon were not equal to the load? You'd say I should have calculated the bulk and weight before starting, and should have taken a larger

Tiling the Low Lands to Perfect Drainage.

wagon and some more mules. That's right. Well, it's just so with a farmer who starts into a season's work with three horses when he really needs four, or possibly five. I

BE SURE YOU HAVE MOTIVE POWER ENOUGH FOR SEASONS WORK

always figure out how much motive power I am going to need and then provide myself and have some to spare, too. Have enough horse power to do the work with ease,

68

then you can crowd your work instead of having the work crowd you.

Better have two idle horses than lack one.

Feel for the horse and don't expect more than he is able to do. Then feed well and keep them fat.

FEED WELL AND KEEP YOUR HORSES FAT

Now, as to the idea that because I farm on a pretty extensive scale I have the advantage of the smaller farmer. It's a mistake

Some More of the Work Teams.

in every way. I only take advantage of modern methods and he is apt to farm like our grand fathers did. Why does he do it? Oh, THE BIG FARMER HAS NO ADVANTAGE OVER THE SMALL ONE I don't know. No other business could stand such neglect and aimless efforts. Just think of a man raising corn year in and year out, never changing the crops, never putting any fertilizer on the land, using old dilapidated implements year after year, half doing his work and getting only half as much as he should from the land.

Where Corn Is Converted Into Prime Beef.

The small farmer can buy feeders just as cheap as I can, he can sell fat stock for just as high prices—ask any commission man if I am not right. A man can make more if he runs a farm that requires several hired men, feeds one hundred or more cattle, with HIRED MEN PAY—DON'T TRY TO DO IT ALL YOURSELF proper number of hogs, etc., than one who does the work himself, and only has a few acres—simply because the profit per acre is somewhere about the same. Of course, the man with a few acres can, FOLLOW THE ADVICE OF THE AGRICULTURAL COLLEGE if he will, make his land produce more an acre by thorough and scientific farming, but the trouble is—we all read enough how it should be done— but few of us do as we are instructed. So you see, the more acres well farmed, the greater returns. Now, I don't mean merely book farming, for I don't do that. I take good care of my men, land and stock. I farm, as suggested by the Agricultural College, in rotation, corn for four or five years, then clover for a few years, and then back to corn, and so on. It takes a carload of clover seed each spring to sow down my land that I am changing from cornfield to meadow. While the land is in grass, I feed cattle on it and let them eat grass and corn and then I haul out manure, all I can. It pays big. You can see the benefit the first crop, and for several succeeding crops. My manure spreaders are really coinage machines, they make money for me. I believe I can combine extensive and intensive farming and make it pay. I know it. I try to make poor land good, and good land better.

ADVANTAGE COMES FROM USING PRESENT DAY METHODS AND NOT FARMING IN FASHION OF FIFTY YEARS AGO

USES CARLOAD OF CLOVER SEED EACH YEAR IN CROP ROTATION

FIRST FARMING ON RIGH,T LINES, THEN FEEDING BY RIGHT METHODS

Mr. Rankin's Favorite Spreader.

Now don't mistake what I mean by extensive farming. I don't mean you have to have a bigger farm than anyone else to make it pay. I do mean you should extend your field of operation. Keep up with the times— widen out. If for years you have been farming 160 acres, try 200, or even more. **Get tools so you can do it and then you will find** some additional gains at the end of the **year.** Raise more corn to feed more cattle and **hogs** to buy more land to raise more corn.

Yes, you can buy land and make it **pay.** Land is cheap as a rule, and I know it to **be** the safest investment, and where any **kind** of judgment is used there is little risk in buying. Keep your earnings invested in land. It is **good** business.

Two of the

Foremen Enroute

to Their

Respective Divisions.

My advise would be to farm all you can, and do the work right; then feed all you raise.

I don't want to give anybody the idea that this story is written with any thought of reflection on antiquity, the people or methods

A Rankin Farm Barn and a Prime Team of Mules, Representing Over $600.00; Weigh 3600 Pounds.

at any time or place in the world, past or present, but rather to express my gratitude for every ray of light that has come to me and other farmers in this, the greatest of all vocations.

My limited knowledge of agriculture indicates that this great enterprise was started and encouraged in Egypt under the Pharaohs. Then agriculture was the AGRICULTURE FIRST STARTED IN EGYPT one calling that brought forth the energies of the people. They had the soil of the Nile valley, and transferred its fertility to food by muscle and sweat of the brow.

In all history the farmer has been first and most important, but he has been afraid to declare his sovereignty until of late years. The old idea that the farmer was ignorant, and a subject for ridicule has become

THE FARMER IS NOT RIDICULED LIKE HE USED TO BE a thing of the past. The fact that the world is dependent upon him is now recognized by everybody, and he is paid the homage which is due.

The user of the reap hook, the cradle, the hoe, and all other original implements have and always will have an honored place in his-

A Rankin Farm House.

tory, and as the ages have rolled away these time honored tools have played their part in broadening the vision of the farmer—helped to make his possibilities unlimited. No, I do not want to throw any slurs at these. They did their part well. But if my life's efforts have in any way helped to keep the farmer abreast with the progress in all other lines of industry, I count my time well spent.

Possibilities! Yes, there is no limit for the farmer, and we do well to tell all we know to the boys and help them to grasp the situation, and to be always looking for means and methods to advance the cause of agriculture. We differ in this from all other business en-

The Finished Product.

terprises, and I am glad of it, too. We try to help each other instead of keeping our means and methods secret. That is one of the good things about farming. It is open and above board. We don't have to discuss plans of operation behind closed doors, with a sentinel at the door.

Think of the farmer's home, overflowing with hospitality and good cheer! He always makes you welcome at any time, and it does not matter what kind of work he is doing, for he knows it is honorable—more than that, it is noble. Even the birds

FARMING IS ONE CALLING IN WHICH THERE IS NO COMPETITION BETWEEN NEIGHBORS

are at home there, and welcome you with glad songs. It is the place of all places for our young men to seek.

Now, to compare methods in the past with those in use now is about the only way I know of getting a correct view of our progress. Who would have ever thought when I was a boy, the farmer would have telephones, pianos, automobiles and all these things which make life so pleasant, to say nothing of the great number of labor-saving devices? When we think of the wonderful things that have been done in the past who would dare to place a limit on the possibilities of the future?

THERE IS NO END TO POSSIBILITIES
ON THE FARM

Yes, I am proud of the Tarkio College. It is my pet of the different enterprises in

Tarkio College. Tarkio, Mo.

which I am interested. Altogether I expect I have given about $200,000 to it, and I believe it is the best investment I have made. The cut shows the main college building and the ladies' dormitory. We are just starting a new dormitory for the young men.

You see, I had no school advantages and I can see where I need education, and I want to have it so any young man or woman can get an education. It takes an educa- tion now to fit the young people for life. I would like to see every boy and girl so equipped with education as to get the best out of every opportunity.

One of the Commissary Wagons for the Feed Lots Loaded with 8,300 Pounds of Champion Molasses Feed Used With Corn and Roughage to Make a Balance Ration.

Let me tell you, the boy that gets an edu- cation nowadays should be instructed as to what to study and why. An education will help them in any calling. Of course, I think the farm is the thing to fit one's self for. While a common school educa- tion might do, higher education is much better. I am sure it will make life more pleasant and useful in many ways. I would impress upon every young person the importance of getting an education. This college is a great achievement for our locality. No, it is not my college. It is "our college." Every one that has helped in any way is a partner, and entitled to part of the credit for success. Its officers and teachers we should appreciate more than we do—not merely those of this college but of all colleges. Their fidelity to their calling is noble and worthy of imitation. I have always felt grateful to the teachers who took so much pains with my boys and girls. It's too bad we don't show our appreciation more for the noble men and women who spend their lives in educating the youth, not only in books, but also in good manners, good morals, honesty, uprightness, etc.

APPRECIATES PAINS AND TROUBLES OF CHILDREN'S TEACHERS

I never will forget my early training, how anxious father and mother were about me. They wanted to have good boys and girls for my playmates. I can see why. And I always did my best to keep my children in good company. It's only too true that a boy or a girl may be judged by the company he or she keeps. Good society and proper training at home and the chances for good boys and girls are in your favor by big odds. That's why I am so interested in colleges. They teach the good things and inspire the young folks for the better things in this life. Every father and mother should lend aid to this means of uplift.

RIGHT BRINGING UP OF CHILDREN THE CROWNING GLORY

To make good farmers of your sons, get them to look up, not down; get them to see the noble side of every question; teach them to love the farm—that's the place that will give more real pleasure than anywhere else.

GIVE THE BOYS AND GIRLS PROPER TRAINING AT HOME

In closing I want to give a little advice to every father and mother, on the farm at least. Give plenty of thought to the cultivation and growth of corn and other crops, but above all give your most faithful attention to the cultivation and growth of your boys and girls so that in your declining years you can look back with pride and see that your family is the greatest of all your achievements.

Don't neglect the proper equipment either. See that the home is comfortable, convenient, pleasant and attractive, for the home of the American Farmer can be really a palace.

And if I can be of assistance to any fellow farmer by giving further infor- ADVICE CHEERFULLY GIVEN TO FARMERS mation about my farm operations, etc., it will be a pleasure to do so, all such inquiries will be answered cheerfully

I am proud of my record as a plain farmer, and what I have accomplished as a farmer in lands, stock, etc. But the one thing that I count as my greatest work is that I have raised four children who are looked upon as honorable, industrious, respected citizens, whom I consider worthy of the confidence of their neighbors and to whom I can leave my life's earnings with full assurance that it will not be used for any questionable purpose.

DAVID RANKIN.

Impressions From Visitors

"Of all the nations of the earth, we stand easily first in the rapidity of soil depletion. David Rankin put the science of soil conservation into practice on his farm in advance of the scientist and teacher. In contrast with the American spirit of gaining wealth at the expense of the soil, Mr. Rankin, with a soil that was new and supposedly inexhaustible, pursued the policy, from the outset, of husbanding its resources that he might hand it over to those who were to follow him unimpaired in productiveness and value. His commandment, the eleventh in the Decalogue of every thrifty farmer, "Thou shalt not sell corn," was inexorable. The writer some years ago put the question directly to him: "Could you not make more money, in some seasons at least, by selling the corn you grow than by feeding it to cattle and hogs," He promptly answered: "Unquestionably. And many times I know this before the feeding operations have begun. This, however, does not alter my practice. What would happen to my land under such a system of farming? I feed all the corn I grow back to my land, and feed also back to my soil as much of the corn grown on my neighbor's land as he will sell me. When I am done with this land I want it to be richer instead of poorer than when I took it as virgin prairie."

"The example of a farmer worth over $3,500,000 who is too poor to pursue the soil robbing system of farming so characteristic of our country and age must stand through all the years as an inspiration to the smaller farmer, helping him to resist the constant temptation to waste the soil he tills."

—*H. J. WATERS, Dean of College o Agriculture, of Missouri*

268

"In the summer of 1903, I was making a tour of the corn belt. No study of the corn belt would be complete without a study of Mr. David Rankin of Tarkio, Mo., and his methods. On coming in sight of Tarkio, one of the most impressive things was a huge quadrangular building, which, upon inquiry, I learned to be Mr. Rankin's barn. Just before entering the town, I passed a large watering trough, fed by an artesian well, near which, as it was noon, a number of men and a small army of mules were taking their noonday meal. In reply to my questions, I was informed that the mules were the property of Mr. Rankin and the men were in his employ. It was corn-plowing time and they had all been at work in the vast cornfield which stretched away out of sight over the neighboring hills. In the afternoon President Thompson, of Tarkio College, undertook to get me an interview with Mr. Rankin, and as Mr. Rankin was just on the point of starting out for a drive over some of his farms, he came around for me, taking me with him for the rest of the afternoon.

As soon as he drove up, I saw that I was in the presence of an unusual personality. He was a man whom anyone would pick out in any company as a great man. His strong, rugged features, massive forehead, bristling eyebrows, the fire of a smouldering energy which glowed in his eyes, all combined to impress the observer with the power and vigor which one associates with a great commander in a military age, or a great captain of industry in an industrial age. Every-

where about his farms were the evidences of his energy and his wisdom. The men were respectful and seemed to be proud to be in his employ. The horses and mules were well fed, and of the very best quality, capable of doing the strenuous work which he demanded of them. The men were well paid, receiving somewhat higher wages than farm hands ordinarily get; but by reason of the good wages, Mr. Rankin had been able to select a better quality of men than the ordinary farmer gets into his employ. And by the use of the best tools and implements, and an abundance of horse-power, he was able to get more work out of his men than the ordinary farmer gets. There was no waste energy. One got the impression that every thing was so organized that every scrap of energy utilized about the farms resulted in something definite and profitable.

These are the impressions which have remained with me during the six years which have elapsed since I visited Mr. Rankin.

—*T. N. CARVER, Professor of Economy, Harvard University.*

"The Missourian is not the only American who wants to be 'shown.' The Eastern man has heard so many marvelous stories about the West that he is apt to take them with considerable salt—until he visits such states as Missouri. Here one sees a standard of agriculture which seems wonderful in contrast with the states east of the Mississippi river and especially the Middle states, since the area of land is so large in proportion to the population to work it. The farmer from the older part of the United States is amazed at the quantity and quality of the harvests, the well kept farm lands and other evidences of progress and prosperity. So many of the small farmers of the East are accustomed to depending on their muscle rather than their brain that to visit such a place as that of David Rankin they could not believe that this man has accomplished such results with human labor he employs.

These are some of the reasons why Mr. Rankin can be called a national educator, if not a benefactor, for his methods in agriculture have been a great object lesson in farming with the brain—employing labor-saving machinery wherever possible in the various processes and the methods of the business man in marketing crops while he has shown the benefit of crop variation, the value of systematic fertilizing of the soil and increase in revenue which may be obtained by introducing new cereals and other staples such as have been advocated by the Department of Agriculture.

In the opinion of an outsider such as the writer, Mr. Rankin's life work has been of the greatest value to the country at large since he has shown how the rural life may be made happy and prosperous, not only for the man of wealth, but for the farmer of small means. When we remember that the majority of our population live without the town and city, we can realize more forcibly what such men as David Rankin mean in our national progress."

—*DAY ALLEN WILLEY, Author and Writer in National Magazines.*

CPSIA information can be obtained
at www.ICGtesting.com
Printed in the USA
BVHW040433160720
583419BV00019B/400